SECRET HISTORY

THE IRAQ WAR

SECRET HISTORY

THE IRAQ WAR

SIMON ADAMS

ARCTURUS

This edition first published by Arcturus Publishing
Distributed by Black Rabbit Books
P.O. Box 3263
Mankato
Minnesota MN 56002

Printed in China

Series concept: Alex Woolf
Editors: Karen Taschek and Alex Woolf
Designer: Tall Tree
Picture researcher: Alex Woolf

Library of Congress Cataloging-in-Publication Data

Adams, Simon, 1955-
    The Iraq War / Simon Adams.
        p. cm. – (Secret history)
    Includes index.
    Summary: "This high-interest series, aimed at reluctant
readers, looks at secret campaigns behind the major
conflicts of the past 100 years. Biographical sidebars
focus on heroic or notorious personalities. Highlighted
fact features include special operations and their results,
resistance movements, propaganda and the history of
the time - as is known....and not readily known"–
Provided by publisher.
    ISBN 978-1-84837-698-4 (library binding)
    1. Iraq War, 2003—Juvenile literature. I. Title.
    DS79.763.A33 2011
    956.7044'3–dc22
                        2010011764

SL000972US   Supplier 03 Date 0510

Picture credits:
Arcturus: 7 (Stefan Chabluk).
Corbis: cover *top left* (Shepard Sherbell), cover *right*
(Mohammed Khodor/Reuters), 6 (Brooks Kraft), 8
(Nameer Noor-Eldeen), 11 (Christophe Calais), 12
(Lance Cpl. James J Vooris-USMC/Reuters), 14 (Olivier
Coret), 15 (Reuters), 16 (Reuters), 25 (Ceerwan Aziz/
Reuters), 26 (Cheryl Diaz Meyer/*Dallas Morning
News*), 27 (David Furst/Pool/epa), 28 (Mohammed
Khodor/Reuters), 29 (Jerome Sessini), 30 (Larry
Downing/Reuters), 31 (Zohra Bensamra/Reuters), 33
(Al Jazeera/epa), 36 (Reuters), 37 (Ali Mohammed/
epa), 43 (Kamal Akrayi/epa).
Getty Images: 9, 10 (Matthew Hannen/USAF), 13
(DigitalGlobe), 17 (Wathiq Khuzaie), 18 (USAF), 19
(Mai/Mai/Time Life Pictures), 20 (Scott Nelson), 22
(Patrick Barth), 23 (Patrick Barth), 24 (Spencer Platt),
34 (Wathiq Khuzaie), 35 (AFP), 38 (Jamal Nasrallah/
AFP), 39 (Justin Sullivan), 40 (David Furst/AFP), 41
(Wathiq Khuzaie), 42 (Wathiq Khuzaie).
Rex Features: 32.
Shutterstock: cover *bottom left* and 21 (Oleg Yarko).

Cover illustrations: *top left*: A poster of Saddam Hussein
from 1995; *bottom left*: An unmanned aerial vehicle
(UAV); *right*: A masked Iraqi insurgent carries a machine
gun during fighting in the town of Falluja (2004).

Spread heading illustrations are all from Shutterstock: 6,
10: F-16 Fighting Falcon aircraft (Ramon Berk); 8: gas
mask (Stephen Mulcahey); 12: satellite (Spectral-
Design); 14, 22, 40: armored troop carrier (yuri4u80);
16, 34: missile launcher (yuri4u80); 18: bomb (fckncg);
20, 28, 30, 36: automatic assault rifle (CreativeHQ);
24, 26, 32: barbed wire (Nikita Rogul); 38: mega-
phone (MilousSK); 42: flag (Juha Sompinmäki).

Every attempt has been made to clear copyright.
Should there be any inadvertent omission, please apply
to the publisher for rectification.

CONTENTS

WAR AGAINST IRAQ

On March 20, 2003, almost 300,000 US-led troops invaded Iraq. In 21 days, the invading armies captured all the major cities in Iraq and overthrew the government of Saddam Hussein, one of the world's most brutal dictators. By May 1, the invasion was over. The United States and its Coalition allies had won. Very soon, however, Iraq descended into chaos as militant groups began attacking Coalition forces and each other. The Iraq War had actually just begun.

On September 12, 2002, President George W. Bush urged the United Nations to take strong action to force Iraq to get rid of its weapons of mass destruction.

WHY THE WAR WAS FOUGHT

President George W. Bush said that Iraq was part of "an axis of evil." He went to war "to disarm Iraq of weapons of mass destruction [WMD], to end Saddam Hussein's support for terrorism, and to free the Iraqi people."

AXIS OF EVIL

On January 29, 2002, President George W. Bush made his annual State of the Union Address to US Congress. He said, "Iraq is a regime that has something to hide from the civilized world." Speaking of Iraq, Iran, and North Korea, he went on to say that "states like these, and their terrorist allies, constitute an axis of evil, aiming to threaten the peace of the world."

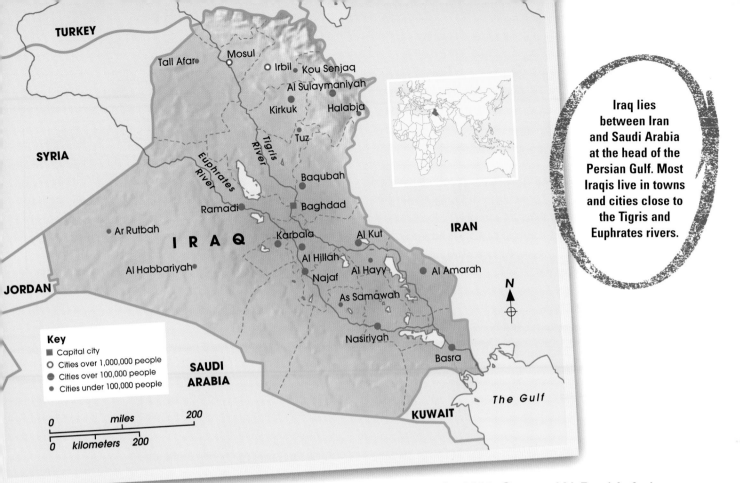

TURKEY
Tall Afar
Mosul
Irbil
Kou Senjaq
Al Sulaymaniyah
Kirkuk
Halabja
Tuz
SYRIA
Tigris River
Euphrates River
Baqubah
Ramadi
Baghdad
Ar Rutbah
I R A Q
Karbala
Al Kut
IRAN
Al Hillah
Al Habbariyah
Al Hayy
Najaf
Al Amarah
JORDAN
As Samawah
N
Nasiriyah
Basra
SAUDI ARABIA
The Gulf
KUWAIT

Key
■ Capital city
○ Cities over 1,000,000 people
● Cities over 100,000 people
• Cities under 100,000 people

0   miles   200
0   kilometers   200

Iraq lies between Iran and Saudi Arabia at the head of the Persian Gulf. Most Iraqis live in towns and cities close to the Tigris and Euphrates rivers.

The United States and its allies believed that Iraq had secret stocks of chemical, biological, and even nuclear weapons that were a threat to world peace. They also accused Iraq of supporting terrorist groups, such as the al-Qaeda group that had attacked targets in the United States on September 11, 2001—9/11—killing nearly 3,000 people. Finally, they wanted to end Saddam Hussein's murderous dictatorship in Iraq.

THE REAL REASONS?

But were these the real or only reasons for going to war? Many opponents of the war believed President Bush wanted to overthrow Saddam Hussein for personal reasons. In 1991, George W. Bush's father, who was president at that time, had attacked Iraq to force it out of neighboring Kuwait, which Iraq had invaded in 1990. Although Iraq was defeated, Saddam Hussein survived and continued to oppose the United States. Others believed that the United States invaded Iraq in order to take control of its vast oil reserves.

IN THEIR OWN WORDS

In November 2002, President George W. Bush declared:

Should Iraqi president Saddam Hussein choose not to disarm, the United States will lead a coalition of the willing to disarm him.

From a speech at a NATO summit in Prague, Czech Republic, November 20, 2002

WEAPONS OF MASS DESTRUCTION

One of the main causes of the war was the world's belief that Saddam was stockpiling weapons of mass destruction (WMD). Iraq had once tried to build a "supergun" (see panel). It had also used mustard gas in its war against Iran from 1980 to 1988 and used both mustard gas and the nerve agent sarin against Kurds in the village of Halabja in 1988.

THE SUPERGUN

In the late 1980s, Saddam Hussein tried to build a "supergun", capable of firing long-range missiles. The gun was 512 feet (156 meters) long, had a three-foot (one-meter) bore (barrel width) and could fire a missile into orbit around the world. In 1990, parts of the weapon were seized in Europe on their way to Iraq, while the rest of the gun was blown up in Iraq by United Nations (UN) weapons inspectors in 1991.

Two Kurdish girls walk through the cemetery at Halabja. Many of the victims of the Iraqi chemical weapon attack of March 1988 were buried here. About 5,000 were killed in the attack, and 10,000 were injured.

After the war against Kuwait, UN weapons inspectors destroyed many WMD, including this 1,100-pound (500-kilogram) mustard bomb.

UN INSPECTIONS

After Iraq's unsuccessful invasion of Kuwait in 1990–1991, UN weapons inspectors found and destroyed large quantities of hidden WMD. When Iraq tried to obstruct the inspectors in 1998, US and British planes bombed Iraq to try to force it to cooperate.

In 2002, under pressure from the UN, Iraq agreed to allow the weapons inspectors to return. The head inspector, Hans Blix, used tips from Iraqis and intelligence information from spies and satellite surveillance to track down possible WMD and the factories that made them. He found little evidence that any WMD still existed. Both the US and British governments disagreed with him.

DRONE ATTACKS

In October 2002, the Central Intelligence Agency (CIA) presented a secret report on Iraqi WMD to the Senate. The report stated that Iraq could fire chemical and biological weapons using unmanned aerial vehicles (UAVs) or drones. The drones could be launched from ships in the Atlantic and hit cities in the eastern United States. These drones did not exist, nor did Iraq possess any WMD. This was confirmed in a report issued in 2005 by the CIA.

IN THEIR OWN WORDS

The US military defines weapons of mass destruction as

Weapons that are capable of a high order of destruction and/or of being used in such a manner as to destroy large numbers of people. Weapons of mass destruction can be high explosives or nuclear, biological, chemical, and radiological weapons.

From *JP 1-02 Department of Defense Dictionary of Military and Associated Terms*, April 12, 2001

A SECRET BASE

The US government always claimed that it had no plans to attack Iraq before 9/11 and that the invasion was part of its campaign against global terrorism. A secret air base in the Persian Gulf state of Qatar suggests a different story.

Engineers use a crane to install an arch during construction of the US air base at Al Udeid in Qatar. It was built in 2001–2002 to create a new base for US forces in the region.

AL UDEID

The official story is that after 9/11, the US government urgently needed to set up a new base in the Persian Gulf. Its main regional base—the Prince Sultan Air Base in Saudi Arabia—was about to close since the Saudis would not allow it to be used for attacks against other Arab nations. The US military needed a new base.

They chose Al Udeid base in Qatar, not far from Iraq, which the Qatari government had begun building in 1996. After October 2, 2001, civil engineers of

IN THEIR OWN WORDS

An engineer of the US 823rd Red Horse Squadron stated in October 2001 that Al Udeid

. . . was nothing more than a runway and a field of sand covered by two-dozen tents and a few warehouses.

Within a year it was the biggest military facility in the Persian Gulf.

www.mydd.com/story/2005/6/21/11741/6199

the 823rd Red Horse Squadron, a specialist unit used to build roads and runways in remote areas, quickly transformed it into the biggest air base in the region, capable of accommodating up to 10,000 troops and 120 aircraft.

THE REAL STORY?

In fact, the United States began to develop the base as soon as George W. Bush became president, in January 2001—eight months before the 9/11 attacks. This work was kept secret and the existence of the base itself denied. What could be the purpose of such a large military base in Qatar? According to some commentators, it proves that the United States was planning an invasion of Iraq long before 9/11.

HUSHED UP

The existence of the Al Udeid base was a closely guarded secret. On October 10, 2001, Master Sergeant "Andy" Andrews died in an accident at the base. His family were not told where he had died, only that it was somewhere in "southwest Asia." They were also not told how he died and had to wait months to find out what he was really doing in the region.

WATCHING THE ENEMY

Before and during the war, the United States used spy planes and satellites to spy on Iraq. They photographed Iraqi military sites, targets, and troop movements. The information they gave to Coalition forces was vital during the invasion.

US Marines prepare to launch a small "Dragon Eye" aerial reconnaissance drone over Fallujah in November 2004. Such drones provided valuable information about enemy activity for US forces on the ground.

PROVOCATION

The single-engine Lockheed U-2 aircraft can fly in all weather at heights of up to 70,000 feet, or 13 miles (21,000 meters). This means it can fly high over enemy territory and take photos without fear of attack from enemy aircraft.

IN THEIR OWN WORDS

When President George W. Bush met British prime minister Tony Blair in January 2003, before the war broke out, he apparently told Blair:

The US was thinking of flying U-2 reconnaissance aircraft with fighter cover over Iraq, painted in UN colors. If Saddam fired on them, he would be in breach [of UN resolutions].

From a memo of a meeting at the White House, Washington, DC, January 31, 2003

During the buildup to the war, the president suggested provoking war with Iraq by painting a U-2 plane in United Nations colors (see panel). If the Iraqis attacked it, they would be in breach of UN resolutions requiring Iraq to disarm. This would then give the United States the right to attack. This proposal, made in January 2003, two months before the war started, was kept secret until news of it leaked out in February 2006.

SPIES IN THE SKY

Just before the war, six US satellites flew over Iraq every hour. These were joined in January 2003 by a new Global Positioning System (GPS) satellite that transmitted accurate locations of enemy targets to the US military. This data was used by US bombers to guide their missiles and smart bombs. GPS data also helped troops find their way through the Iraqi desert and guided them around enemy towns.

SPY SATELLITES

The United States uses six types of spy satellites. Optical satellites use a large mirror to gather light for photographs of the ground below. Infrared and ultraviolet satellites record invisible light from below. Radar-imaging satellites use microwave signals to peer through cloud cover. Combined satellites use all the above techniques to provide a more detailed picture of the ground below. Signal-intercept-and-detection satellites tune in to radio, telephone, and data broadcasts. Ocean observation satellites spy on ships at sea. In addition, a network of GPS satellites provides accurate mapping and navigation data.

INVASION AND OCCUPATION

In the days leading up to the invasion, Coalition troops assembled in Kuwait. Preparations for war were kept secret so as not to alert the Iraqis. US Special Forces, in the country since July 2002, helped Kurdish rebels opposed to Saddam Hussein prepare for war. They also identified possible targets for US attack. US bombers attacked targets in the southern part of the country.

In the first few weeks of the war, US bombers regularly pounded Baghdad in a campaign known as "Shock and Awe." Targets included military and security installations.

THE IRAQI ARMY

It is not known how many troops defended Iraq against invasion. The best estimate is about 375,000 soldiers, 20,000 airmen and 2,000 sailors. There were also 44,000 paramilitaries, 80,000 elite Republican Guards, and perhaps 650,000 reservists.

FALSE INFORMATION

A US intelligence agent working as a diplomat in Iraq sold false "top secret" information about the invasion to the Iraqis. These plans suggested that the invasion would come from Turkey or

An Iraqi throws a stone at a statue of Saddam Hussein in Baghdad as US troops pull it down in April 2003. Iraqis later danced on the fallen statue as they rejoiced at the ending of Saddam's 24-year rule.

Jordan, not Kuwait. The Iraqi military believed the information was true and put large numbers of troops in the west and north of the country, away from the actual invasion in the south.

On March 19, 2003, US forces bombed the al-Dora farm buildings south of the Iraqi capital Baghdad. They had received intelligence that Saddam Hussein was visiting his family there. The information was false—Saddam was not present.

ATTACK!

The next day, the war began. US air strikes hit Baghdad. Coalition troops poured into Iraq from Kuwait. On March 23, they fought a massive battle near the southern city of Nasiriyah. British commandos launched an amphibious assault from the Persian Gulf to seize Basra and the surrounding oil fields. In the north, Kurdish rebels attacked Iraqi troops around Kirkuk. On April 9, US troops occupied Baghdad. By May 1, most of Iraq was in Coalition hands. Coalition troops had won the war, but they did not achieve peace. Saddam loyalists, Iraqi nationalists, and Islamic fighters took up arms against the occupying troops and then began to fight each other. Within weeks, Iraq was close to civil war.

WEAPONRY

Although the two sides in the war were roughly matched in terms of troop numbers, the military advantage lay with the invading forces. Coalition troops were better trained and equipped and had far better morale than their Iraqi counterparts. Above all, they had better weapons.

THE HUMVEE

The Humvee—high-mobility multipurpose wheeled vehicle—was the main transportation used by Coalition troops in Iraq. More than 10,000 were used to carry troops and equipment, operate as weapons platforms, and serve as ambulances. Because of their high ground clearance, they are able to ford up to 2.5 feet (0.8 meters) of water. There are 17 different types of Humvee. The latest model is protected by hardened steel and bullet-resistant glass, making it ideal for use in urban warfare.

During the invasion, Humvees were used by US Army Special Forces to secure a key area south of the city of Najaf in central Iraq.

SUICIDE BOMBERS

A suicide bomber is a person who uses a bomb or another explosive device to kill or injure others, knowing that he or she will die in the process. The most common methods are to drive a car loaded with explosives and blow it up in a public place, such as a market square or a mosque, or to strap bombs to the bomber's own body and detonate them next to the target. It is not known how many suicide bombings have taken place in Iraq since the invasion, but they number in the thousands, with 478 attacks in 2005 alone.

An Iraqi woman walks past the burned-out remains of a suicide car bomb in Baghdad on November 12, 2006. Two people were killed and seven injured in the attack.

IRAQI FORCES

The Iraqi army was less well equipped. Much of its weaponry was old or out-of-date, and its army put up little fight. After the invasion, however, Iraqi insurgents looted army weapon stores, acquiring large quantities of guns, grenades, and explosives.

The insurgents developed improvised explosive devices (IEDs), homemade bombs placed by the side of the road and triggered by remote control or trip wires when a vehicle or foot patrol passes. They also used suicide bombers (see panel above) and car and truck bombs.

COALITION POWER

Coalition forces were equipped with the latest high-tech weaponry. Stealth (see pages 18–19) and other bombers dropped "smart bombs" that were guided to their targets by the satellites of the Global Positioning System (GPS). US submarines fired computer-guided Tomahawk missiles. US planes fired cruise missiles that were guided by GPS with pinpoint accuracy to their targets. Ground troops used the latest heavily armored and highly mobile tanks, a wide range of mobile and static artillery, and the all-purpose Humvee (see panel on page 16).

BOMBING BY STEALTH

During the invasion of Iraq, the US Air Force (USAF) carried out top-secret bombing missions against military and political targets inside Iraq. The missions were carried out by B-2 Spirit "stealth" bombers, one of the most secret planes in service today.

THE FLYING WING

Most airplanes consist of a fuselage (the tube-shaped body), two wings, and a tail. The wings give the aircraft its lift. The B-2 Spirit stealth bomber is a completely different design: it has one big wing, shaped like a boomerang. This is much more efficient because, instead of separate wings supporting the fuselage, the entire craft works to create lift. With no fuselage and tail, there is also less air resistance, allowing it to travel farther and faster than ordinary planes.

A B-2 Spirit stealth bomber in flight. The aircraft is designed to penetrate enemy anti-aircraft defenses and deploy both bombs and missiles.

INVISIBLE TO RADAR

The B-2 Spirit bomber is designed to be almost impossible for enemy radar to detect in flight. Its unique, "flying wing" design has few sharp edges that can be picked up by radar. Its engines are buried within its wing so that they give out few detectable exhaust fumes. Its non-metallic composition and special paint coating both absorb (rather than reflect back) radar signals sent from the ground. Due to these different stealth technologies, the plane gives out few acoustic (sound), infrared, visual, or radar signals in flight. This helps the plane avoid enemy detection and allows it to penetrate air defences and attack its targets.

SECRET MISSIONS

Everything about the B-2 is top secret. The planes that bombed Iraq flew from an undisclosed "forward operating location," as well as from the B-2's home base at Whiteman Air Force Base in Missouri and from the Indian Ocean island of Diego Garcia. The targets the planes hit are also secret, but it is known that they dropped 1.5 million pounds (680,000 kilograms) of bombs, including 583 "smart bombs" guided to their targets by the GPS satellites.

A USAF aerial tanker refuels a B-2 Spirit stealth bomber in flight. Aerial refueling greatly extends the B-2's range and also allows it to take off with a larger bomb payload.

LONG-DISTANCE FLIGHTS

The B-2 Spirit can travel up to 6,800 miles (11,000 kilometers) without refueling. However, by refueling in mid-flight, the plane can fly from its base in Missouri to Iraq and back, a total distance of about 14,260 miles (23,000 kilometers).

SPECIAL FORCES

During the invasion of Iraq, the regular ground and air forces commanded most of the public's attention. But working alongside them were special forces from the United States, the UK, and Australia. These highly trained soldiers conducted secret and dangerous missions deep inside enemy territory.

A US Army Special Forces team carries out a raid to capture one of the leaders of a pro-Saddam militia movement, the Saddam Fedayeen, in August 2003.

INSIDE IRAQ

Even before the invasion began, US Special Forces helped Kurdish rebels fight the Iraqi army in the north. In the west, about 80 men from the Australian SAS (Special Air Service) were dropped into western Iraq alongside British SAS troops, a battalion of British Royal Marines, and US SOFs (Special Operation Forces). Their role was to prevent Iraq from firing Scud missiles, which had happened in the 1991 Gulf War. In fact, no such missile sites remained. The troops stayed behind enemy lines for 42 days, taking prisoner about 2,000 Iraqi Republican Guards and special forces.

IN THEIR OWN WORDS

One special forces officer operating in the deserts of western Iraq called it a "Special Forces playground" since they had the area to themselves and could run riot. They were praised by Coalition commander General Tommy Franks:

They have accomplished some wonderful things out there.

Quoted in Nigel Cawthorne, *Inside the Elite Forces* (Robinson, 2008)

Unmanned aerial vehicles were used extensively by Coalition forces during the Iraq War to fly over enemy territory and take photographs.

SEIZING AIRFIELDS

On the second day of the invasion, combined special forces seized two airfields close to the western border with Jordan. The airfields were used as bases for ground reconnaissance missions against enemy targets identified by unmanned Predators (see panel). As the special forces headed east toward Baghdad, they received air support from UK Harrier fighters based in Jordan. A third air base was captured in a nighttime parachute assault by members of the US Army's 75th Ranger Regiment.

MQ-1 PREDATOR

The MQ-1 Predator is an unmanned aerial vehicle (UAV), or remote-controlled aircraft. It has been used by the US Air Force since 1995 both as a spy plane and to fire missiles at enemy targets. Cameras on board the aircraft send real-time video images to the ground-based "pilot." During the invasion of Iraq, some older Predators were used as decoys to encourage Iraqi air defenses to expose their positions by firing. From 2003 to 2009, Predators flew thousands of missions over Iraq. Among their key targets were insurgents firing rockets and mortars into Baghdad's Green Zone (international zone).

THE BATTLE OF DEBECKA PASS

While Coalition troops fought major battles around Basra and Fallujah in southern Iraq, a little known battle was being fought in the north. This battle did not involve large numbers of troops and was kept secret at the time since it involved special forces. It was crucial to the Coalition's success.

As part of their operation in the Kurdish areas of northern Iraq, paratroopers of the US 173rd Airborne Brigade secure the Hareer air base near Arbil on March 29, 2003.

THE KURDS

The Kurds live in a region known as Kurdistan, which occupies parts of Iraq, Syria, Turkey, and Iran. The Kurds have a distinctive language, culture, and identity. They have engaged in a long struggle for independence against Turkey and Iraq. They were therefore natural allies of the Coalition against Saddam Hussein.

THE CROSSROADS

On April 4, 2003, US Green Beret troops were told to secure a vital crossroads near the town of Debecka in northern Iraq. If they took the crossroads, they would be able to stop the Iraqi army from moving north into Kurdistan and destroying the oil fields around Kirkuk.

Iraqi Kurds celebrate the liberation of their capital, Kirkuk, on April 10, 2003. Kurdish guerrillas and US Special Forces took the city against little resistance from the occupying Iraqi army.

The 26 troops in the operation landed east of Kirkuk and linked up with the Kurdish Peshmerga militia at Arbil. Once they seized the crossroads, they would have to hold it until they were relieved by the US 173rd Airborne Brigade artillery unit.

FIREFIGHT

Unfortunately, they had no intelligence on local Iraqi forces. The troops soon found themselves in a massive firefight with Iraqi troops who were hiding behind a ridge. The Iraqis were equipped with T-55 tanks and were protected by minefields and trenches. The Coalition troops called in B-52 bombers to smash enemy positions, but then more Iraqi reinforcements arrived and the operation seemed to be headed for disaster.

JAVELINS

The Coalition troops were saved by their portable Javelin anti-tank guided missiles. (The missile is ejected from the launcher and flies a safe distance away before its main rocket motor ignites and blasts the missile onto its target.) The Javelins destroyed six Iraqi personnel carriers before US Navy Tomcat bombers pounded enemy positions. The Iraqis eventually withdrew and the crossroads was taken. It was an important but unreported victory.

IN THEIR OWN WORDS

The Green Berets fought blind at Debecka. As one of their commanders said:

No one knew what was on the ridge line or behind it.

Captain Eric Wright, commander of Operational Detachment A 391, quoted in Nigel Cawthorne, *Inside the Elite Forces* (Robinson, 2008)

SECRET PRISONS

Saddam Hussein was president of Iraq from 1979 until his overthrow during the US-led invasion in 2003. He was a brutal dictator, holding on to power by force and imprisoning and torturing anyone who opposed his rule.

Lahib Norman was a prominent Iraqi lawyer who was imprisoned and tortured under Saddam Hussein. In April 2003, following the regime's downfall, she returned to the prison where she had been held.

TORTURE

During Saddam's 24-year reign, tens of thousands of Iraqis, especially Kurds in the north and Shia Muslims in the south, were tortured and killed in his prison cells. Victims were placed in solitary confinement and were subjected to regular beatings. They were suspended by their hands before being beaten, burned, and given electric shocks. Days before the 2003 invasion, Saddam announced a general amnesty for almost all Iraqi prisoners and the jails were emptied.

PROTECTING SADDAM

Two main organizations protected Saddam Hussein. The paramilitary People's Army was responsible for internal security and protected him against any attempted army revolt. The Mukhabarat, or Iraqi Intelligence Service, led by Saddam's half brother Barzan Ibrahim al-Tikriti, gathered international intelligence but was also involved in killing and torturing political opponents at home.

ABU GHRAIB

One of the most notorious prisons in Iraq was in the city of Abu Ghraib. The prison held up to 15,000 inmates, many of them Kurds and Iraqis of Iranian background who had been held in the prison without being charged since the Iran-Iraq war of 1980–1988. Many were tortured and executed—101 prisoners were shot on just one day, December 10, 1999.

After the US-led invasion, Abu Ghraib was brought back into use by US forces to house convicted prisoners. The 372nd Military Police Company of the US Army ran the prison. In 2004, journalists in the United States revealed that Iraqi prisoners in Abu Ghraib had been subjected to physical, psychological, and sexual abuse, including torture and rape, by their guards. The stories caused international outrage and did immense harm to the image of the US-led administration in Iraq.

ASSASSINATION

Saddam's intelligence services regularly assassinated his opponents at home or in exile abroad. In 1993, the Iraqi Intelligence Service attempted to assassinate former president George Bush and the emir of Kuwait with a large car bomb. The bomb went off, but both men escaped unharmed. In response, the US government fired 23 cruise missiles at the Intelligence Service headquarters in Baghdad.

In May 2004, US troops guarding Abu Ghraib prison were confronted by crowds of women demanding to know whether their relatives held inside were safe. The women were worried that they might have been tortured by the US prison guards.

CAPTURING SADDAM

When Coalition forces entered Iraq, one of their main aims was to capture Saddam Hussein, dead or alive. They expected this would be an easy task. After all, it was difficult for Saddam to remain hidden since everyone knew his face. Yet he evaded capture for almost nine months.

Saddam Hussein's hiding place was a small hole in a farmyard in ad-Dawr. He was captured by US troops in Operation Red Dawn on the evening of December 13, 2003. He did not resist.

THE ACE OF SPADES

The United States drew up a list of most-wanted members of the Saddam regime. They printed them as a pack of playing cards to help their troops identify the wanted men. Saddam was at the top of the list as the ace of spades. His sons Qusay and Uday were the aces of clubs and hearts.

WHERE IS HE?

In the months following the invasion in March 2003, various sightings of Saddam Hussein were reported. None were confirmed. Tips from friendly Iraqis led nowhere. Tape recordings of his voice urging Iraqis to resist the invaders were released. In July 2003, Saddam's sons Qusay and Uday, and his 14-year-old grandson Mustapha were killed in a gun battle with US forces, but it was feared that Saddam had either died or gone into exile.

OPERATION RED DAWN

The breakthrough came on December 13, 2003. Troops from the US 4th Infantry Division, working with Task Force 121, an elite Special Operations team, searched two sites in ad-Dawr near Tikrit, close to Saddam's birthplace. At 8:30 p.m. they discovered Saddam hiding in a hole in the ground. He had grown a long beard and was armed with a pistol and an AK-47 assault rifle and had $750,000 in cash with him. He put up no resistance.

After he was captured, Saddam was put on trial, and on November 5, 2006, he was found guilty of crimes against humanity. He was sentenced to death and executed by hanging on December 30.

On November 5, 2006, Saddam Hussein was found guilty of crimes against humanity and sentenced to death. He shouted at the judge as the verdict was read out.

IN THEIR OWN WORDS

In his last letter, written shortly after his death sentence, Saddam wrote:

Many of you have known the writer of this letter to be faithful, honest, caring for others, wise, of sound judgment, just, careful with the wealth of the people and the state . . . and that his heart is big enough to embrace all without discrimination.

Quoted from a letter written by Saddam Hussein in November 2006

GUERRILLA WARFARE

When Coalition forces invaded Iraq, they expected to fight the Iraqi army and the elite Republican Guard in pitched battles. Instead, the Iraqi army largely collapsed, with many soldiers either refusing to fight or surrendering to advancing Coalition troops. In the insurgency that followed, Coalition troops were faced with an enemy that adopted the classic techniques of guerrilla warfare.

IRREGULAR FIGHTING

Guerrilla warfare consists of small groups of irregular troops—soldiers who do not form part of a regular army—conducting surprise attacks on enemy positions. Guerrillas avoid pitched battles since they rarely have the numbers or equipment to take on a fully equipped army. Instead they conduct rapid raids, ambush enemy troops with bombs and booby traps, and fight in unexpected ways.

AZ ZUBAYR

British troops advancing toward Basra in southern Iraq in the first days of the war found themselves fighting an unseen,

An Iraqi celebrates as a US Army Humvee is set alight, following a shoot-out between US forces and guerrillas in Fallujah in March 2004.

ORIGIN OF THE TERM

The word *guerrilla* means "little war" in Spanish. It first came into use in the Peninsular War of 1807–1814 between France and Spain, when small groups of irregular Spanish fighters attacked the occupying French army. The guerrillas disrupted French supply lines and carried out small-scale attacks against isolated French soldiers, helping to drive the French out of Spain by 1814.

Guerrilla warfare was particularly fierce in and around the city of Fallujah in central Iraq. Here US Marines take up position in the northeast part of the city in November 2004, during Operation Phantom Fury.

secret army of former and current Iraqi soldiers, rebels and Saddam loyalists, and religious extremists. The guerrillas were equipped with mortars, rocket-propelled grenades, anti-aircraft guns, and Kalashnikov AK-47 assault rifles.

The fighting was particularly intense around Az Zubayr, a small town south of Basra. One British soldier was killed in an ambush while another two, both members of the Royal Engineers, were seized while on a mine-clearing mission and later killed. Snipers attacked the incoming British troops, who fought their way into the town house by house. The town was eventually secured, but fighting here was a foretaste of what was to occur throughout Iraq.

IN THEIR OWN WORDS

Lieutenant Chris Broadbent of the British Black Watch infantry regiment fought in Iraq. He said:

The original brief had changed completely. Before we came out [to Iraq], we believed that if we were going to do any fighting it was going to be in the open, but they were using guerrilla tactics.

Quoted in Nigel Cawthorne, *On The Frontline* (John Blake Books, 2009)

THE INSURGENCY

In just three weeks, Coalition forces toppled Saddam Hussein and freed Iraqis from his brutal rule. They expected to be welcomed as liberators but were met instead by a largely hostile population. Within weeks, armed militias had formed and were fighting back. The insurgency had begun.

MISSION ACCOMPLISHED

On May 1, 2003, President Bush addressed the crew of the aircraft carrier USS *Abraham Lincoln* as the ship returned from Iraq. He said: "In the battle of Iraq, the United States and our allies have prevailed." In the background, a large banner stated "Mission Accomplished." It is not known who put that wording on the banner, but it returned to haunt the president in the years that followed as the insurgency grew in strength.

The banner of May 1, 2003, declared that the mission was "accomplished," but despite President Bush's confidence, fighting continued in Iraq throughout the rest of the decade.

RELIGIOUS CONFLICT

Some Iraqis who took up arms against the Coalition were loyal to Saddam and wanted him back in power. Others were nationalists who hated the occupation and wanted all foreign troops out of Iraq. At least 12 major and 40 smaller groups took part in the insurgency. Many of them were secretive, shadowy groups that used a variety of different names to conceal their identities. Some were foreign fighters, including members of al-Qaeda, who wanted to spark an Islamist war against the invaders.

The two major groups of insurgents were drawn from Iraq's main religious communities. Iraq is a largely Islamic country. About a third of Iraqis follow Sunni Islam, in common with most of the Islamic world. Two-thirds follow Shia Islam, the minority branch of Islam followed in Iran. Saddam Hussein had ruled Iraq through its Sunni minority, persecuting the Shia majority.

CIVIL WAR

With Saddam gone, Sunnis fought to protect their status as the governing group against the Shi'a as well as resisting the US-imposed government. The main fighting took place in the "Sunni Triangle," an area northwest of Baghdad. Sunnis attacked Shia mosques, killing hundreds. Shia Muslims fought back to

An Iraqi Shia militiaman holds up a rocket-propelled grenade launcher in the town of Kufa, close to the Shia sacred city of Najaf.

protect their own people and gain control of the country. The insurgency was eventually defeated by Coalition and Iraqi troops in 2007–2008, although fighting continued for a long time after that.

THE DEATH TOLL

Up to 130,000 fighters were involved in the insurgency. It is not known exactly how many were killed, but the number is probably around 24,000, with roughly the same number captured by Coalition forces.

KIDNAP!

On September 16, 2004, three men were seized in the al-Mansour district of Baghdad. Kenneth Bigley, Eugene Armstrong, and Jack Hensley were civil engineers working for Gulf Supplies and Commercial Services, which was helping to rebuild Iraq after the invasion.

Kenneth Bigley was born in Liverpool, UK, and worked in Iraq as a civil engineer before he was taken hostage in September 2004.

THE DEMAND

The three men were kidnapped by the Tawid and Jihad group led by terrorist Abu Musab al-Zarqawi. On September 18, the group released a video. It showed the three captives kneeling in front of the group's banner. The message was clear and deadly. If the United States and Britain did not release all Iraqi female prisoners within 48 hours, the three men would be killed.

IN THEIR OWN WORDS

On September 22, 2004, Kenneth Bigley pleaded with British prime minister Tony Blair on a video released by his kidnappers:

I need you to help me now, Mr. Blair, because you are the only person on God's earth who can help me.

From a video posted on an Islamist website, September 22, 2004

THE OUTCOME

When the deadline expired, Eugene Armstrong was beheaded. One day later, Jack Hensley was also beheaded. Despite the release of the only two female Iraqi prisoners held by the Coalition, Kenneth Bigley was also beheaded on October 7. The deaths sent shockwaves around the world.

HOSTAGE TAKING IN IRAQ

Hostage taking was common in Iraq after the invasion. Coalition troops and civilian workers were often kidnapped by groups involved in the insurgency but were usually released in return for money. The Tawid and Jihad group, later known as al-Qaeda in Iraq, were different. They were religious fanatics. Their aim was not to raise money but to force an end to Western occupation and create a pure Islamic state in Iraq.

Between 2004 and 2009, over 200 foreigners and thousands of Iraqis were kidnapped. Of these, dozens were killed. Many were seized for ransom. Others, however, were taken simply to raise awareness of a cause and create a climate of fear.

Among the many foreign hostages seized in Iraq were two German engineers, taken in January 2006. Their captors threatened to kill them unless Germany closed its embassy in Baghdad and its companies withdrew from Iraq. The two were released unharmed in May.

MARGARET HASSAN

Margaret Hassan was the head of Iraqi operations for CARE, the humanitarian relief organization. On October 19, 2004, she was kidnapped in Baghdad. In a video released by the kidnappers she pleaded for the withdrawal of British troops. Despite international demands for her release, she was killed and her body was found on November 15. The kidnappers were never identified.

33

THE IRANIAN CONNECTION

In 2005, US forces in Iraq became aware of a new, secret enemy. The insurgency was at its height, mostly led by Sunni militants and Saddam loyalists in the western part of Iraq. But this enemy came from the east.

In July 2007, a US military explosives expert displayed explosives and bombs used by Iraqi militants that had been manufactured in neighboring Iran. The weaponry included an Iranian-made armor-penetrating roadside bomb.

IRAQ AND IRAN

For years, Iraq and Iran had been enemies. In 1980–1988, the two countries fought a brutal war in which at least a million people died. The Iranian government was hostile to Saddam Hussein and was glad to see him toppled in 2003. During the insurgency that followed, Iran—the leading Shia Muslim

IN THEIR OWN WORDS

It is true that weapons clearly, unambiguously, from Iran have been found in Iraq.

Speech by Secretary of Defense Donald Rumsfeld at a Pentagon press conference in Washington, DC, August 9, 2005

state—secretly supported the Iraqi Shia militias in their struggle against Sunni militias and the occupying forces. By this means, Iran hoped to extend its influence in Iraq.

THE QUDS FORCE

Iran supported the Shia militias through the Quds Force, a special unit of Iran's powerful Revolutionary Guard that operates in different countries. In Iraq, the Quds Force was run by Abu Mustafa al-Sheibani and consisted of a network of secret agents. According to US intelligence sources, the Quds Force supplied, organized, trained, and financed Shia militias such as the Badr Brigade.

It equipped them with roadside bombs, rocket-propelled grenades, and Katyusha rockets, which were then used against Coalition forces.

A NEW WEAPON

The Quds Force introduced a new and deadly type of roadside bomb to Iraq. The bomb contained shaped, explosive charges that could pierce a tank's armor. At least 37 such bombs were detonated against Coalition forces in Iraq in the first half of 2005 alone, with the loss of many lives.

THE TALON

Talon robots were used by US forces in Iraq to move and dispose of live grenades, bombs, and other explosives that were too dangerous for humans to handle. These small, light robots are easily transported and instantly ready for use. A solider operates a Talon with a digital control unit that directs its movements from a safe distance.

A Talon robot gets ready to defuse a roadside bomb in Iraq in July 2008. Remote-controlled Talons reduce the risk to bomb disposal experts as well as saving the lives of those who might have been killed the bomb had gone off.

TASK FORCE BLACK

During the insurgency, many terrorists made Baghdad their base. They attacked troops and other military targets, bombed buildings, launched suicide car bomb attacks against civilians, and disrupted gas and other supplies. A special unit, known as Task Force Black, was set up to defeat these terrorists.

A car bomb explodes outside a restaurant in a Shia neighborhood in southern Baghdad in July 2007. Task Force Black succeeded in greatly reducing the number of such attacks.

SECRET FORCE

Task Force Black was a highly secretive unit. It consisted of special forces from the British SAS and the US counterterrorist 1st Special Forces Operational Detachment—Delta, known as Delta Force. The task force started work in summer 2006, when car bombers were killing about 3,000 people a month in Baghdad. They performed a series of "black ops"—top-secret operations done without official authorization so the Coalition authorities could, if necessary, deny responsibility.

IN THEIR OWN WORDS

General David Petraeus, head of US forces in Iraq, was full of praise for the SAS:

They have exceptional initiative, exceptional skill, exceptional courage and, I think, exceptional savvy. I can't say enough about how impressive they are in thinking on their feet.

Interview in the *Times*, August 14, 2008

A group of around 30 suspected al-Qaeda members are led blindfolded through a military detention center in Baghdad in November 2007, following a military operation in the area.

SUCCESS

Task Force Black used intelligence from spies and informers to take about 3,500 terrorists off the streets of Baghdad in 18 months. Most were arrested. Several hundred, however, who were members of al-Qaeda, were shot.

The task force achieved great success. They broke up the terrorist network in Baghdad and helped reduce the number of bombings from about 150 a month in 2006 to just two by summer 2008.

AL-QAEDA

Al-Qaeda is a global network of Sunni Islamic militant groups founded in 1989 by Saudi Arabian–born terrorist Osama bin Laden. It aims to overthrow Western-supporting regimes in the Muslim world and replace them with pure Islamic states. To achieve its aim, al-Qaeda carries out terrorist attacks. Its most infamous attack was against the United States on 9/11, when suicide bombers crashed planes into the World Trade Center in New York and the Pentagon in Washington, DC. After the 2003 invasion of Iraq, members of al-Qaeda moved into the country. Their aim was to force the withdrawal of Coalition forces, topple the Coalition-supporting Iraqi government, and establish a Sunni Islamic state.

PROPAGANDA

The Iraq War was conducted in the full glare of the world's news media. Events were constantly reported on television, radio, and newspapers around the world. Both sides in the conflict tried to manipulate the media to get their views across and undermine the enemy. Both sides used propaganda.

MISINFORMATION MINISTER

Mohammed al-Sahhaf was the Iraqi Information Minister during the 2003 invasion—the official voice of the Saddam regime. He became famous for his laughably inaccurate announcements about how the war was going. On April 7, he claimed that there were no US troops in Baghdad and that the Americans were committing suicide by the hundreds at the city's gates. In fact, US tanks were in Baghdad, just a few hundred yards from where he was standing.

In his last public appearance on April 8, 2003, al-Sahhaf announced optimistically, the Americans "are going to surrender or be burned in their tanks."

لا تجازفوا بحياتكم

وبحياة رفاقكم

US warplanes dropped bombs filled with propaganda leaflets over Iraq in the buildup to the invasion in 2003. The leaflets aimed to discourage the Iraqis from fighting the invading Coalition forces.

SADDAM'S PROPAGANDA

Before the invasion, Saddam Hussein and his regime used propaganda to promote his image as an all-powerful leader, declaring that Iraq would destroy Coalition forces if they dared to attack. However, once the invasion got under way, Saddam's propaganda machine fell apart and little was heard from him.

COALITION PROPAGANDA

The invasion of Iraq was not popular and ignited fierce protests in many parts of the world. Coalition propaganda therefore aimed to convince people back home that this was a just war against a brutal enemy. To help achieve this, restrictions were placed on media reporting.

Journalists were "embedded" within an army unit. They could go where the unit went and were protected by them. However, it is difficult to criticize soldiers if you are relying on them for protection.

INSURGENCY PROPAGANDA

The Iraqi insurgents used propaganda to spread fear and undermine people's faith in the Coalition forces and the Iraqi government. They used low-tech methods such as graffiti slogans, leaflets, and newsletters. They also produced DVDs and even established an Arabic-language television station to get their message across. Hostage takers used the Western media to put pressure on governments to make concessions.

IN THEIR OWN WORDS

Lt. Col. Rick Long of the US Marine Corps was asked why the military decided to embed journalists with the troops:

Frankly, our job is to win the war. Part of that is information warfare. So we are going to attempt to dominate the information environment.

Jeffery Kahn, "Postmortem: Iraq War Media Coverage Dazzled But It Also Obscured," *UC Berkleley News*, March 18, 2004

THE SURGE

By 2006, it was clear that the Coalition was losing the war against the insurgents in Iraq. Civil war was raging in many parts of the country, and Coalition troops were being killed in large numbers. The US government would not withdraw its troops since that would be to admit defeat.

US soldiers taking part in the surge establish positions in the Dora neighborhood of southern Baghdad—part of an operation to clear the city of insurgents.

MORE TROOPS

On January 10, 2007, President Bush decided to send in a "surge" of extra troops to swamp the enemy and reduce violence in the country. More than 20,000 troops were sent, mainly to Baghdad. They went to support the Iraqi army in clearing the insurgents out of the city. In addition, 4,000 marines and increased numbers of Special Forces were sent to Anbar province in western Iraq where al-Qaeda

IN THEIR OWN WORDS

In a televised address to the American people in January 2007, President Bush announced:

America will change our strategy to help the Iraqis to carry out their campaign to put down sectarian violence and bring security to the people of Baghdad. This will require increasing American force levels.

From a televised address from the White House Library, Washington, DC, January 10, 2007

was particularly active. A large part of the new strategy, led by General David Petraeus, was to win the hearts and minds of the majority of Iraqis by building relationships and creating a feeling of security, thereby isolating the extremists.

The first troops began to arrive at the end of January. At first the surge did not work. The monthly death toll in Iraq rose 15 percent from February to March 2007. Three months after the surge began, US troops controlled less than one-third of Baghdad.

US TROOP NUMBERS

In March 2003, 248,000 US troops invaded Iraq. That number fell to around 160,000 in December 2005 and 133,000 the following March. During the surge in 2007, 28,500 more arrived, but the total number then fell back again as the surge ended, to around 130,000 in July 2009.

SUCCESS

During the summer, however, the surge began to have an impact. Secret intelligence led to the capture of the leaders of an Iranian-backed Shia group, while other Shia militias were disrupted and broken up. Violence between Sunni and Shia groups began to decrease, and civilian deaths from car bombs also fell. People in Baghdad started to feel safer, and normal life resumed at last. The success of the surge brought the end of US involvement in Iraq closer.

As the surge took effect and the insurgency quieted down in 2008, normal life began to return to large parts of Iraq. Here a group of Iraqi girls enjoy a day out in Baghdad's zoo, an activity that would have been impossible during the previous five years of fighting.

CONCLUSION

By 2010, Iraq was very different from the way it was back in 2003. Saddam Hussein had gone, most of the Coalition troops had left, and a new, democratic government was in charge. But was Iraq now at peace?

A US colonel shakes hands with his Iraqi opposite number as Coalition troops hand over control of Baghdad's high-security Green Zone to the Iraqis on January 1, 2009.

POLITICAL CHANGES

The invasion of 2003 ended Saddam's 24-year rule. The Coalition Provisional Authority took power and tried to rebuild the country. After a year, it handed over control to the Iraqi Interim Government. Peaceful democratic elections were held in January 2005, although many Sunnis refused to vote. The National Assembly drafted a constitution that was signed in October 2005.

IN THEIR OWN WORDS

On January 1, 2009, US troops handed over control of Baghdad's Green Zone to the Iraqi government. Prime Minister al-Maliki said:

This palace is the symbol of Iraqi sovereignty and by restoring it, a real message is directed to all Iraqi people that Iraqi sovereignty has returned to its natural status.

From a speech at the Republican Palace, Baghdad, January 1, 2009

Two months later another election took place, this time with Sunnis joining in. Nouri al-Maliki, a Shia, became prime minister, with Jalal Talabani, a Kurd, as president. The new government slowly gained respect as it tackled Iraq's many problems.

An Iraqi Kurdish woman votes in the regional elections held on July 25, 2009. Slowly and steadily, a culture of democratic government is being established in Iraq.

TROOPS OUT

The success of the 2007 surge meant that the insurgency died down in 2008. Of the 40 Coalition nations that took part in either the invasion or the occupation, most had withdrawn by the end of 2008. Britain and Australia withdrew in 2009. The United States handed over control of all cities to the newly formed Iraqi army in June 2009 and agreed that all remaining US troops would leave by the end of 2011.

Yet violence, car bombings, shootings, and kidnappings continued to occur every day. Iraq remained a nation divided between Shia and Sunni and between a brutal past and—it is hoped—a peaceful future. The war was not over yet.

THE DEATH TOLL

By June 2009, 4,646 Coalition soldiers had been killed in Iraq—4,328 of them Americans and 179 British. Between 6,370 and 10,800 Iraqi troops died during the invasion. Another 11,525 Iraqi Security Forces died between 2003 and 2009 and possibly 24,000 insurgents. Between 100,000 and 150,000 Iraqi citizens died in the war, although the exact figure is not known. Most died during the height of the insurgency in 2006–2007.

43

TIMELINE

July 2002 US Special Forces first enter Iraq.

March 19, 2003 US bombers attack al-Dora farm complex.

March 20, 2003 Invasion begins with attacks on Baghdad and amphibious assault on Basra and the oil fields.

March 23, 2003 US troops fight a major battle at Nasiriyah.

April 6, 2003 British troops take Basra.

April 9, 2003 US troops occupy Baghdad.

April 10, 2003 US and Kurdish troops occupy Kirkuk.

April 21, 2003 The Coalition Provisional Authority (CPA) is established.

May 1, 2003 President Bush states that the US invasion has been successful.

July 22, 2003 Saddam's two sons are killed in a massive fire-fight.

December 13, 2003 Saddam Hussein is captured by US troops.

June 28, 2004 The CPA hands over power to the Iraqi Interim Government under Iyad Allawi.

October 7, 2004 British hostage Kenneth Bigley is beheaded.

October 19, 2005 The trial of Saddam Hussein begins.

December 15, 2005 The New National Assembly is elected; a new government is formed under Nouri al-Maliki.

December 30, 2006 Saddam Hussein is executed after he is found guilty of crimes against humanity.

January 10, 2007 President Bush announces surge of extra troops to put down insurgency.

May 31, 2009 Last British troops leave Iraq.

44

GLOSSARY

ally A country that agrees to support and work with another country.

al-Qaeda A loose-knit global network of Sunni Islamic militant groups founded in 1989 by Osama bin Laden and responsible for a number of major terrorist attacks around the world.

amphibious assault A military attack launched from the sea.

coalition An alliance of countries working and fighting together for a common purpose. The Coalition attacking Iraq in 2003 consisted of the United States, UK, Australia, and Poland, with another 36 countries involved at some stage of the operation.

commando A member of a military unit trained to make swift raids into enemy territory or against enemy positions.

Congress The lawmaking assembly of the United States, consisting of the House of Representatives and the Senate.

constitution A written document setting out the principles on which a country is governed and the rights its people enjoy.

cruise missile A computer-guided missile powered by a jet engine that can carry a nuclear or conventional warhead over a long distance.

democracy A system of government where the leaders have been elected freely by all of its citizens or a country with such a system.

dictatorship Government by a leader who rules with absolute power, usually by force.

firefight An intense battle between two heavily armed groups.

guerrilla A soldier who is not part of a regular army and fights by means of ambush and hit-and-run attacks.

hostage A person who is held prisoner by a person or group until demands made by his or her captors are met.

infantry Soldiers who fight on foot.

insurgency A revolt against the government of a country.

irregular forces Fighters who are not part of an organized army.

kidnap Capture and hold a person.

militia An armed force of trained civilians who are not part of a regular army.

nationalist Someone who is loyal or devoted to his or her country.

nuclear weapons Bombs or missiles that release nuclear energy to create a massive explosion—for example, an atom bomb or hydrogen bomb.

paramilitary A member of a military group similar to or modeled on the regular army but not belonging to it.

propaganda The organized and deliberate attempt to control news, information, and ideas to persuade an intended audience to think or act in a certain way.

SAS Special Air Service, an elite British special forces group.

special forces Military groups that have been trained to operate behind enemy lines and use guerrilla tactics.

terrorist Someone who uses violence to achieve political ends.

United Nations (UN) An organization representing the world's nations that tries to resolve international crises and promote world peace.

weapons of mass destruction (WMD) Chemical, biological, or nuclear weapons capable of inflicting great loss of life.

FURTHER INFORMATION

BOOKS
Adams, Simon. *Eyewitness Soldier*. Dorling Kindersley, 2009.

Barker, Geoff. *Changing World: Iraq*. Franklin Watts, 2008.

Cawthorne, Nigel. *On the Frontline: True Stories of Outstanding Bravery by British Forces in Iraq and Afghanistan*. John Blake, 2009.

Cawthorne, Nigel. *The Mammoth Book of Inside the Elite Forces*. Robinson, 2008.

Mason, Paul. *Timelines: The Iraq War*. Franklin Watts, 2010.

WEBSITES
www.bbc.co.uk/history/recent/iraq

iraq.usembassy.gov/

www.mideastweb.org/iraq.htm

www.pbs.org/newshour/indepth_coverage/middle_east/iraq/

INDEX

Page numbers in **bold** refer to illustrations.